LIFE
CYCLES

by
Grace Jones

Photocredits
Abbreviations: l-left, r-right, b-bottom, t-top, c-centre, m-middle.

Front Cover – Romain JL. 2 – Noradoa. 4t – kazoka. 4bl – vvoe. 4br – kazoka. 5tr – Oksana Kuzmina. 5br – Andresr. 5b – Edyta Pawlowska. 5bl – mimagephotography. 5tr – LeventeGyori. 6t – ilikestudio. 6bl – Pan Xunbin. 6bc – Henrik Larsson. 6br – Pan Xunbin. 7t – Cathy Keifer. 7b – Anneka. 8t – LeAnnMarie. 8b – Mathisa. 9t – Antoine Beyeler. 9b – MarkMirror. 10 – Girish HC. 11tr – Henrik Larsson. 11br – Cathy Keifer. 11bl – dossyl. 11tl – Nicola Gordon. 12t – Don Mammoser. 12b – Ian Grainger. 13tl – vvoe. 13tr – prajit48. 13b – Adwo. 14t – Michiel de Wit. 14b – KWSPhotography. 15r – Ricardo de Paula Ferreira. 15bl – Dr. Morley Read. 16 – clearviewstock. 17t – Peter Baxter. 17tr – Manfred Ruckszio. 17br – Manfred Ruckszio. 17bl – Michiel de Wit. 17tl – USBFCO. 18t – Maciej Olszewski. 18b – Lehrer. 19t – yaibuabann. 19b – Waugsberg (distributed under a CC 2.5 license, via Wikimedia Commons). 20 – kowit sitthi. 21t – jocic. 21b – ffolas. 22 – Igor Podgorny. 23tr – Shaiith. 23br – Lehrer. 23bl – Roman Pyshchyk. 23tl – Michael Nivelet. 24tl – dariazu. 24tr – Ian 2010. 24b – antpkr. 25t – surassawadee. 25b – Bogdan Wankowicz. 27 – Zoom Team. 28 – KaKrue. 29tr – Jiri Hera. 29br – surassawadee. 29bl – Zeljko Radojko. 29tl – pkproject. 30t – Eric Isselee. 30ml – Rosa Jay. 30mr – jocic. 30bl – yevgeniy11. Images are courtesy of Shutterstock.com. With thanks to Getty Images, Thinkstock Photo and iStockphoto.

©2017
Book Life
King's Lynn
Norfolk PE30 4LS

ISBN: 978-1-78637-042-6

Written by:
Grace Jones

Edited by:
Charlie Ogden

Designed by:
Drue Rintoul

CONTENTS

Words in **bold** are explained in the glossary on page 31.

WHAT IS A LIFE CYCLE?

All living things go through changes and different stages of development from the beginning to the end of their lives. Together, these changes are called a life cycle. Some living things have only a few simple stages in their life cycle, whilst others have many complex changes that occur before they can reach **adulthood**.

Some animals, such as frogs, undergo an extreme process of change called metamorphosis. This means that during their life cycle their whole body structure changes; for example, frogs grow front and back legs, develop lungs and lose their tails.

A YOUNG FROG, CALLED A TADPOLE.

A FULLY GROWN, ADULT FROG.

See how much you have changed in your lifetime by looking at the human life cycle below. Which stage of the life cycle are you at?

FOETUS

HUMANS START LIFE AS AN UNBORN BABY, CALLED A FOETUS, GROWING IN THEIR MOTHER'S **WOMB**.

BABY

A BABY IS BORN AFTER SPENDING AROUND NINE MONTHS DEVELOPING IN THEIR MOTHER'S WOMB.

OLD AGE

CHILD

ADULT

A TEENAGER DEVELOPS INTO A FULLY GROWN ADULT.

AT THIS STAGE A HUMAN LEARNS TO WALK AND TALK.

ADOLESCENT

CHILDREN CONTINUE TO GROW AND BECOME TEENAGERS.

LIFE CYCLE
OF A BUTTERFLY

WHAT IS A BUTTERFLY?

A butterfly is an insect. Insects are animals that have six legs and usually one or two pairs of wings. Most insects, including butterflies, are cold-blooded animals. This means that their body temperature changes with the temperature of their environment.

BUTTERFLY

LAYING EGGS

During the first stage of a butterfly's life cycle, an adult female butterfly searches for a plant to lay her eggs on. She sticks her eggs to the plant's leaves with a glue-like substance that she produces naturally. Butterfly eggs are usually oval or circular in shape and can be extremely varied in their colour and size.

BUTTERFLY EGGS

A female butterfly can lay up to 100 eggs at a time.

HATCHING CATERPILLARS

After around two weeks of growing, the butterfly **embryo** has developed into a caterpillar, or larva, and it is ready to hatch. The caterpillar hatches by breaking its eggshell and then wriggling its way out.

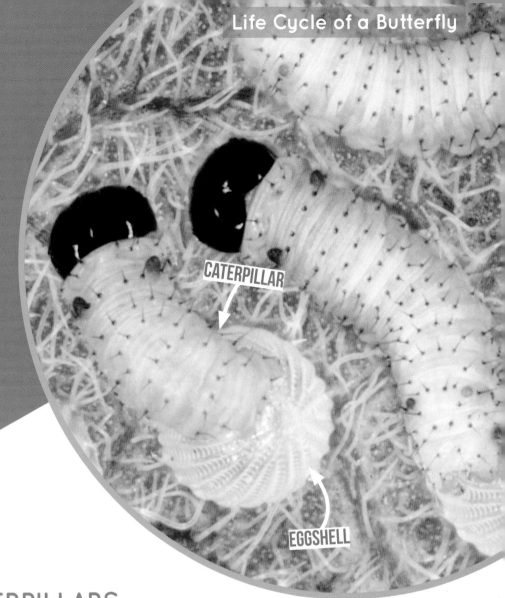

CATERPILLAR

EGGSHELL

GROWING CATERPILLARS

The newly hatched caterpillar will eat its own eggshell, the leaf it hatched on and the leaves around it. It needs to eat lots of food because of the amount of energy it requires to continue to grow and change. It grows so quickly that its skin becomes too small for its body; it sheds its tight skin and grows a new, bigger skin underneath.

Caterpillars will have eaten around 27,000 times their own body weight by this stage of their life cycle.

CATERPILLAR SKIN

7

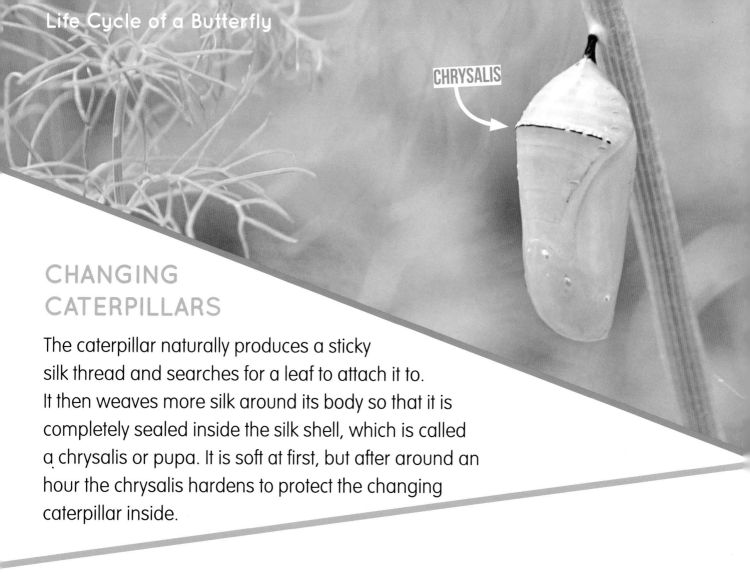

CHRYSALIS

CHANGING CATERPILLARS

The caterpillar naturally produces a sticky silk thread and searches for a leaf to attach it to. It then weaves more silk around its body so that it is completely sealed inside the silk shell, which is called a chrysalis or pupa. It is soft at first, but after around an hour the chrysalis hardens to protect the changing caterpillar inside.

CHRYSALIS TO BUTTERFLY

Inside the chrysalis, the caterpillar's body begins the process of metamorphosis by breaking down its body into a liquid and then reforming it as a butterfly's. It grows two pairs of wings, two **antennae** and its mouth grows into a straw-like tongue. After around two weeks, the chrysalis shell breaks open and an adult butterfly **emerges**.

PROBOSCIS

LOOKING FOR FOOD

All adult butterflies are **herbivores**. Most butterflies drink the nectar found in the flower heads of plants for their food. Some absorb other liquids, such as the sap found on trees, the liquid found in rotting fruit, wet sand and mud. Butterflies absorb all kinds of liquid through their long, thin proboscis (tongues), which act as straws.

BRILLIANT BUTTERFLIES

Many butterflies stand out because of their colourful and patterned wings. Their bright colours trick predators into believing that they are poisonous and dangerous. This keeps them safe and stops them from being eaten by other animals.

SEARCHING FOR A MATE

Once an adult butterfly has emerged from its chrysalis, it is ready to search for a mate so that it can **reproduce**. A male butterfly seeks out a female of the same species by sight. He recognises her by the size, colour and shape of her wings.

If the female accepts the male, the male grasps onto the back of her body using clasping organs. They join the tips of their **abdomens** and the male **fertilises** the female's eggs by releasing a liquid into her body. After mating has finished, the male flies away and the female searches for a leaf to lay her eggs on.

ABDOMEN

LIFE CYCLE OF A BUTTERFLY

ADULT BUTTERFLY

EGGS

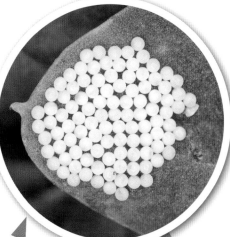

A FEMALE BUTTERFLY LAYS HER FERTILISED EGGS ON THE LEAF OF A PLANT.

A FULLY GROWN ADULT BUTTERFLY EMERGES FROM THE CHRYSALIS.

CHRYSALIS OR PUPA

CATERPILLAR

A CATERPILLAR BEGINS ITS METAMORPHOSIS INSIDE THE CHRYSALIS THAT IT HAS CREATED.

A CATERPILLAR HATCHES FROM A SINGLE EGG.

LIFE CYCLE OF A FROG

WHAT IS A FROG?

A frog is an amphibian. Amphibians are animals that can live both in water and on land. All amphibians, including frogs, are cold-blooded animals. This means that their body temperature changes with the temperature of their environment.

A female frog can lay up to 20,000 eggs at a time.

LAYING EGGS

The first stage of a frog's life cycle begins when a female frog lays her eggs – called frogspawn – in freshwater (normally in a pond or river). Each egg has a tiny, black tadpole embryo inside the jelly-like substance that surrounds it. For around two weeks the small embryo grows by eating this jelly-like substance for food and energy.

JELLY

EMBRYO

FROGSPAWN

HATCHING TADPOLES

After around two weeks of growing, the tadpole embryo has developed a head, tail and gills. It is now ready to hatch. It wriggles out of the frogspawn using its long, strong tail, which also helps it to swim quickly when it is out in the open water. The tadpole uses its gills to breathe in **oxygen** from the water.

GILLS

TAIL

GROWING TADPOLES

Tadpoles eat tiny green plants called algae as food. A tadpole needs to eat lots to provide enough energy for it to continue to grow and change. For around five weeks, the tadpole will eat the algae that grows naturally in its habitat before moving on to the next stage of its life cycle.

ALGAE

CHANGING TADPOLES

As the tadpole grows bigger its body begins a process of metamorphosis. It first grows back legs and then front legs, all while its tail begins to shrink. It then starts to grow lungs, meaning that it can swim to the surface of the water and breathe fresh air. The tadpole has now changed into a **froglet**.

FROGLET TO FROG

The froglet can live in water and on land because it can breathe oxygen in the air through its two lungs or oxygen in the water through its gills. This means that it has become **amphibious**. Its tail keeps shrinking until it eventually disappears. After three weeks, the froglet will have changed into a fully grown adult frog.

There are over 4,000 known species of frog in the world.

LOOKING FOR FOOD

Nearly all adult frogs are **carnivores**. They mostly eat insects, worms, slugs and even small mammals like mice. They use their super sense of smell to hunt out prey during the night, which they catch using their extremely long, sticky tongues.

FANTASTIC FROGS

The Glass frog is around 2cm long. If you look at its body from below, you can see inside of it. Have a look at the picture. What can you see inside the Glass frog below?

THE BRAZILIAN TREE FROG IS THE ONLY KNOWN SPECIES OF FROG TO EAT FRUIT AND BERRIES.

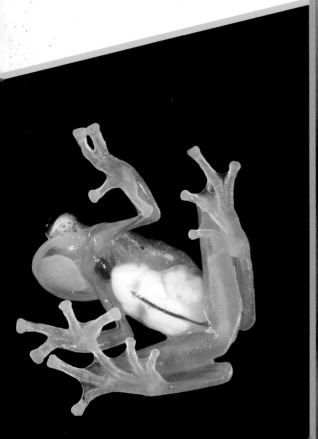

A group of frogs is called an 'army'.

15

SEARCHING FOR A MATE

When an adult frog is around three years old, it is ready to search for a mate to reproduce with. Usually, a male frog attracts a female frog by making loud croaking sounds. These are made by breathing air in and out of a pouch in the frog's mouth, called a vocal sac.

Once a male frog has attracted a female, they climb into the water to mate. The female lays her eggs in the water and the male fertilises them by releasing a liquid over them. The new parents leave their fertilised tadpole embryos in the water to develop on their own.

VOCAL SAC

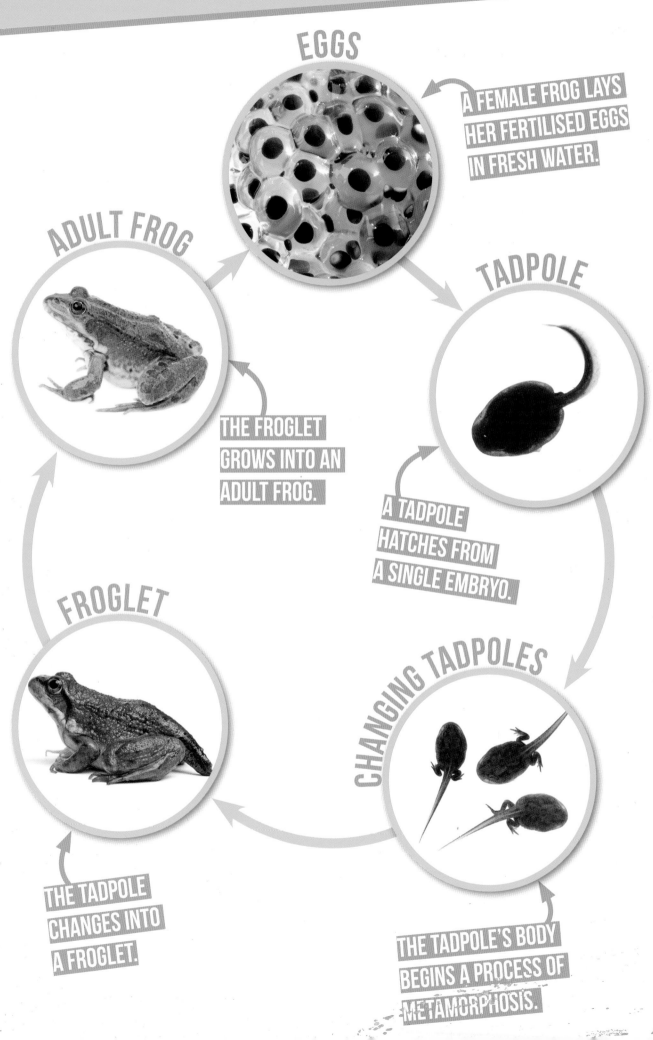

EGGS

A FEMALE FROG LAYS HER FERTILISED EGGS IN FRESH WATER.

ADULT FROG

TADPOLE

THE FROGLET GROWS INTO AN ADULT FROG.

A TADPOLE HATCHES FROM A SINGLE EMBRYO.

FROGLET

CHANGING TADPOLES

THE TADPOLE CHANGES INTO A FROGLET.

THE TADPOLE'S BODY BEGINS A PROCESS OF METAMORPHOSIS.

LIFE CYCLE
OF A HONEY BEE

WHAT IS A HONEY BEE?

A honey bee is an insect. Insects are animals that have six legs and usually have one or two pairs of wings. Most insects, including bees, are cold-blooded animals. This means that their body temperature changes with the temperature of their environment.

LAYING EGGS

One at a time, a **queen bee** lays a single egg on a ball of pollen and wax inside a cell of the beehive. The queen keeps the eggs – and herself – warm by sitting on each cell and quivering her muscles.

CELLS

A queen bee can lay up to 1 million eggs in her lifetime.

LARVA

HATCHING GRUBS

After around four days of growing, the bee embryo is ready to hatch. A small, white grub, called a larva, emerges from each egg. Immediately after it has hatched, the larva eats the pollen ball underneath it to give it energy to grow.

ROYAL JELLY

GROWING GRUBS

For three days the larva is fed on **royal jelly** that the worker bees make. After this, the larva is fed on a mixture of pollen and nectar, known as bee bread. It grows so quickly that its skin gets too tight for its body; it eventually sheds it and grows a new, bigger skin underneath. A grub sheds its skin three times at this stage of its life cycle.

CHANGING GRUBS

Once the larva has sufficiently developed, its individual cell is capped with wax by worker bees. The larva spins a cocoon made of silk around its body so that it is completely sealed inside.

GRUB TO HONEY BEE

Inside the cocoon, the larva sheds its skin one more time before its body begins a process of metamorphosis. The eyes, legs, wings and fine hairs that cover a bee's body begin to develop. After around ten days **pupating**, an adult honey bee chews its way through the wax capping and emerges out of its cell and into the hive.

LOOKING FOR FOOD

All adult honey bees are herbivores. They eat the nectar and pollen that is collected by worker bees from the flowers of plants. Worker bees carry pollen back to the hive in special pollen baskets on their back legs. They absorb nectar through their long, thin proboscis (tongue), which acts as a straw.

POLLEN BASKET

BRILLIANT BEES

Honey bees make the sweet honey that we can buy in shops. It is made from the nectar that the worker bees collect from flowers. Once stored in a honeycomb cell it naturally thickens into honey as water **evaporates** from it. The worker bees then cap the honeycomb cell with wax and start all over again.

REPRODUCTION

The queen bee lays a number of fertilised eggs in special, bigger cells called queen cups. Queen larvae are fed on royal jelly for the whole of their development. When the young queens, called **virgin queens**, emerge from their cells they try to sting and kill one another until only one is left alive.

Six days later, the one surviving virgin queen leaves the hive to mate with around 10–15 male **drone bees**. One at a time, the drones insert a liquid into her body. She stores this and releases it over the next two to seven years of her life whenever she needs to fertilise and lay more eggs.

As many as 21 virgin queens have been counted in one hive.

QUEEN BEE

EGGS

THE QUEEN BEE LAYS AN EGG IN A SINGLE CELL OF THE BEEHIVE.

ADULT HONEY BEE

A HONEY BEE EMERGES FROM THE PUPA.

PUPA

THE GRUB'S BODY BEGINS ITS METAMORPHOSIS INSIDE THE COCOON IT HAS CREATED.

GRUB

A GRUB OR LARVA HATCHES FROM THE EMBRYO.

LIFE CYCLE
OF A SUNFLOWER

WHAT IS A SUNFLOWER?

A sunflower is a tall, thin plant that is **native** to North America and is a member of the daisy family. Sunflowers have large flower heads (around 20cm wide) with yellow, red or orange petals on them.

SUNFLOWER SEED

A sunflower seed is blown by the wind or carried by an insect from a flower head into soil on the ground. The seed becomes buried and stays in the soil until spring. The seed needs warmth from the sun and water from the rain to help it to grow.

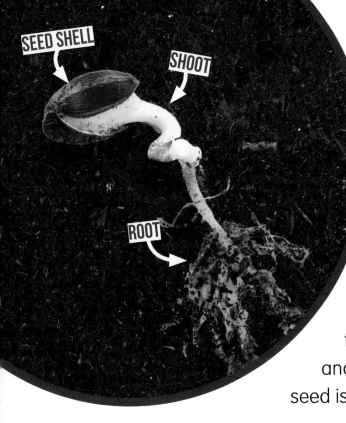

SEED SHELL

SHOOT

ROOT

ROOTS AND SHOOTS

If the seed has enough warmth and water, it will eventually split open so that a tiny root can emerge and begin to grow down into the soil. The root is the part of the plant that absorbs essential minerals, nutrients and water from the soil. Shoots will also begin to sprout from the seed and grow upwards. When roots and shoots start to grow from a seed the seed is said to have germinated.

Remember, roots grow downwards into the soil and shoots grow upwards into the air.

GROWING ROOTS AND SHOOTS

After around two weeks, the tiny **seedling** pushes up and out of the soil in order to try and find sunlight above ground. More shoots may begin to grow from the seedling and more roots will also grow down into the soil to anchor the plant in the ground.

STEM

The long, thin part of a sunflower that grows above the ground is called a stem. Sunflower stems have to be strong to support the plant as it grows taller and heavier. The stem carries water, nutrients and minerals from the roots to the rest of the plant. It also carries food from the leaves to other parts of the plant.

LEAF

FOOD IS CARRIED DOWN FROM THE LEAVES TO OTHER PARTS OF THE PLANT.

STEM

WATER, NUTRIENTS AND MINERALS ARE CARRIED UP FROM THE ROOTS TO THE REST OF THE PLANT.

ROOTS

LEAVES AND BUDS

As the seedling grows taller, leaves start to grow from the shoots of the plant. Leaves absorb **carbon dioxide** from the air and energy from the sun to make the plant's food. This process is called photosynthesis. Buds also begin to grow at the top of the stem, as this is the part of the plant where a flower will begin to grow.

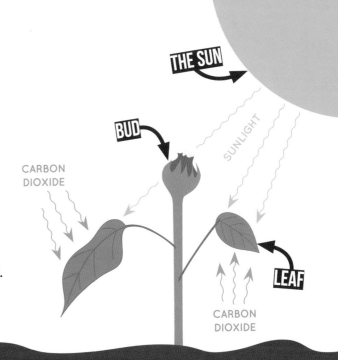

THE SUN

BUD

SUNLIGHT

CARBON DIOXIDE

LEAF

CARBON DIOXIDE

SEED TO SUNFLOWER

After around eight weeks of growing, the sunflower bud will begin to open. Inside each flower head are many other tiny flowers called disc florets. The petals around the disc florets are called ray florets and can be yellow, red or orange.

DISC FLORETS

RAY FLORETS

REPRODUCTION

Once the sunflower plant has flowered (which usually happens in the summer) it produces pollen and nectar that many insects drink. The pollen from the plant is carried to other sunflower plants on the bodies of insects as they search for more food. When an insect touches the pollen against another plant's **stigma**, the plant is said to have been pollinated.

An available egg in the plant is fertilised by the pollen and grows into a seed. Sunflower seeds can be found in the flower heads of sunflower plants. They are carried away by insects or get blown by the wind to become buried in soil.

LIFE CYCLE OF A SUNFLOWER

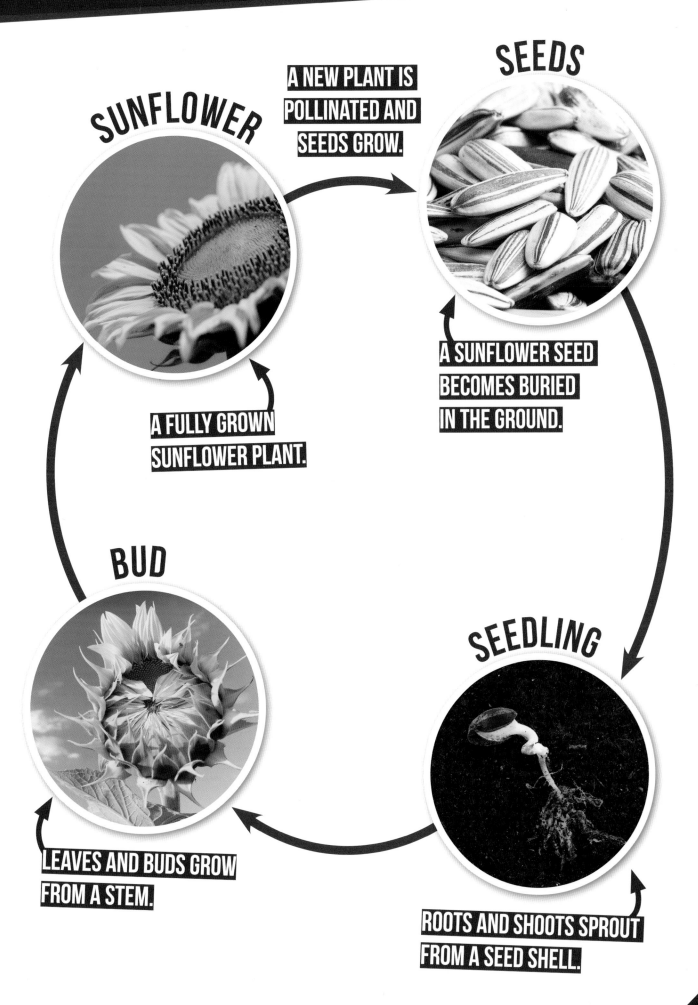

SUNFLOWER

A NEW PLANT IS POLLINATED AND SEEDS GROW.

SEEDS

A FULLY GROWN SUNFLOWER PLANT.

A SUNFLOWER SEED BECOMES BURIED IN THE GROUND.

BUD

SEEDLING

LEAVES AND BUDS GROW FROM A STEM.

ROOTS AND SHOOTS SPROUT FROM A SEED SHELL.

WORLD RECORD BREAKERS

THE WORLD'S FASTEST BUTTERFLY:

The Skipper butterfly, with a top speed of 30 miles per hour. That's faster than any Olympic runner.

THE HIGHEST JUMPING FROG:

The Bullfrog, with a maximum jump height of 2.2 metres – recorded at the Calaveras County Fair in America.

THE WORLD'S LARGEST BEEHIVE:

Over 6 metres long – found in Texas, U.S.A.

THE WORLD'S TALLEST SUNFLOWER:

9.17 metres tall – grown in Kaarst, Germany. That's almost twice the size of the world's tallest giraffe!

GLOSSARY

abdomens	the parts of bodies that contain reproductive and digestive organs
adulthood	the stage in a living thing's life when it is fully grown
amphibious	able to live on land and in water
antennae	a pair of long thin sensors found on the heads of insects
carbon dioxide	a natural, colourless gas found in the air
carnivores	animals that feed on other animals
drone bees	male bees whose job it is to mate with the queen bee
embryo	an unborn or unhatched young in the process of development
emerges	appears or becomes visible
evaporates	loses moisture
fertilises	causes an egg to develop into a new living thing
froglet	a young frog that has recently developed from a tadpole
herbivores	animals that feed on plants
native	a plant or animal that naturally lives in a particular location
oxygen	a natural gas that all living things need to survive
pupating	the act of becoming a pupa
queen bee	a female bee – she is the only one who can produce young in any one hive
reproduce	to produce young through the act of mating
royal jelly	a substance made by worker honey bees and fed to larvae
seedling	a young plant
stigma	the part of a plant that receives pollen and where germination takes place
virgin queens	queen bees that have not yet mated with a drone
womb	the organ in the body of a woman where a foetus develops

INDEX